THE ECLIPSE OF SCHOOL TORMENT!

A Guide to End School Bullying

ARLENE J RAMSEY

authorHOUSE®

AuthorHouse™
1663 Liberty Drive
Bloomington, IN 47403
www.authorhouse.com
Phone: 1 (800) 839-8640

Published by AuthorHouse 01/31/2019

ISBN: 978-1-5462-7820-7 (sc)
ISBN: 978-1-5462-7821-4 (e)

Library of Congress Control Number: 2019900925

From a conqueror of school torment, I dedicate this book to the families of the youths that has taken their own lives as an end result of torment. I also dedicate this book to the youths that are currently experiencing torment, may you suffer in silence no longer!

Torment, also known as bullying, is the imbalance of power used in extremity to intimidate and oppress others. This includes repetition of unwarranted aggressive and or passive aggressive behavior used in various forms such as verbal, physical, social, non-verbal, or cyber by a student or group of students directed towards a student or group of students that has been targeted with the intention to distress, harm, or assassinate the character or social status of the target.

My Experiences with torment:

My 3rd grade year of school, I noticed a pattern from a peer who made it obvious that she didn't like me and told other peers to not associate with me anymore, i was 8 years old at the time and we were all in the 3rd grade. Actually, this happened right after my grandmother took permanent custody of my sister and i. By the time I got in the 4th grade, the temperament of my peers' attitude towards me and how they perceived me changed drastically and that was the crux, from my understanding at that time, of the torment, gaslight and mobbing I was forced to deal with from my middle childhood years through most of my adolescence years. Looking back now at how this all began, I understand how me being bi-cultural, having been raised in a violent community and how the sexual, verbal and physical abuse I've endured at home had such a negative impact on me, how my temperament changed and how this, in many ways contributed to why those children targeted and tormented me. Due to having to cope with such adversity which were concurrent and because of my cultural differences, I became greatly misunderstood by my peers.

From this point on, life at school for me was exasperating. There were so many rumors that were told about me, that to this day, I don't know what half of them were. However, I knew someone or a few were spreading lies about me because I was always singled out. Children approached me everyday, several times a day wanting to know why I "said" something about them or something about someone else, or why did I "do" something to them or someone else. Other times, they didn't question me about what was said to them however, their actions were verbally disrespectful, hostile, combative and wanted to physically fight. To me, this all was devastating because at one point, I was a student who got along with everyone in my class and got along with students that weren't in my classroom. Hence, I couldn't understand how children I was at a point in good relations with, can have disdain and hatred for me without seeing me actually do or say anything to harm them or anyone. I mean, let's go back a few years. In kindergarten, I was the student that helped the teacher by passing out supplies to the class, I passed out the oatmeal and graham crackers, etc.. I befriended every and anyone. During my preschool years, there was an elder Caucasian man who I befriended because he'd be outside in the morning by himself and seemed melancholy every morning. At least, that's what I thought at such a young age. After becoming happy to see each other, he'd give me the 10 lollipops that were connected by clear plastic every morning and every day I got to preschool I shared lolli's with 9 of my peers. I never came home with a lollipop! You know, I kept that same energy and spirit as I progressed to higher grades. Therefore, I couldn't understand why it was so easy for my peers to rival me. At first, I wanted to talk things out because I wanted to know why my peers were confronting me. For one, i rarely got clear and direct answers as to why they confronted me with such hostility and second my peers refused to talk things out and resolve whatever they thought the issue was. Then, this animosity escalated to mobbing on the school bus. Children gathered in cliques in the middle and back of the bus would throw crayons and other things at me rapidly and until there weren't any more crayons in their boxes to throw at me. They would also spit balls in my hair. I wondered why the bus driver never intervened. Needless to say, I have taken my concerns to school administration numerous times in hopes that the adults in leadership at school could find a way to help me and talk to my peers in a way that they understand the harm of their actions. However, from my observation, no one made a firm and consistent effort to stop what have been taking place. At this time, i began taking matters into my own hands for my own safety. I started sitting in the back of the bus in the very last row of seats. From this position, I was able to see who initiates throwing the crayons at me, who was equally antagonistic, eagerly waiting for the opportunity to start mischief and who were the followers. However, from the position that I was sitting they had to turn around to face me in order to throw their crayons for one and second, I learned that they didn't want me to see them throwing crayons at me.

I've also learned that they were more ruthless when they could "throw the stone, hide their hands."

However, due to lack of better disciplinary action from school admin, the mobbing against me escalated to the classrooms and in other areas within the school building. When this happened, I was relieved at first because I understood that administration would now see that I was not the initiator of the problem. Prior to, I was questioned and even spoken to in a way as if I was at fault and that I was the reason why my peers tormented me because they weren't there to witnessed when it began, how it began and with whom it began. Here goes, the antagonism and name calling continued in the classroom. I was told by the teacher to ignore it and nothing was said to the student that was antagonizing me. I ignored it however, it didn't stop. When other students witnessed this, they chimed in on the mobbing during class in the middle of our teacher's presentation. I recall the teacher advising the students to stop interrupting class however, their tone wasn't firm enough and they did not provide a great reason to those students as to why their behavior was unacceptable. Hence, the attacks became an everyday activity until I began to stand straight up and speak up for myself and with rage. And having not been given the proper self-advocacy tools, I did so in the way of shouting, pointing my fingers at people and used profanity. A couple of shifts took place after this. The teacher made it very clear that I am not to disrespect his class again and he instructed me to control my temper. His tone of voice and facial expressions told me that he was in no way understanding of how I felt and how what my classmates were doing has affected me. From his response, i also thought that he thought that I should not speak up for myself and that to ignore what was happening to me was the best thing that I could do despite witnessing that I've ignored previous attacks which resulted in further disrespect and torment from my peers. His response also gave my peers the green light to continue to disrespect and torment me in class, creating more of an imbalance and leaving me with no support or way of being protected by school administration. Because now, they understood that they did not have to wait until lunch recess or after school, my peers had the freedom and confidence to get away with this type of behavior anywhere and at any time of the day. I Also noticed that the peers who were still my friends at this time, disassociated themselves from me which left me further alienated. I guess their understanding was that if the teacher did not help Arlene, something must be wrong with Arlene, she must be the one that is wrong and they did not want to become the next target.

The more I advocated for myself, the more they became annoyed with me and wanted nothing to do with me. Next, I was labeled a trouble maker and noticed unpleasant attitudes from school administration which were expressions of their disappointment and disgust of me. Being sexually and physically abused at home and having no support or protection at home along with what I have been coping with at school? It was at this point in my young life that I have lost all HOPE of ever being protected and supported from school leadership as well as at home. I was left with no choice but to defend myself by any means necessary, I also made it known that my sister was not to be touched. When they realized that the girls could not physically beat me, they got help from the boys at school and there was always a gang of children throwing things at me, kicking me, spitting spit balls in my hair and antagonizing me. My eye glasses were stolen from my desk and still, the teacher didn't make a firm attempt to stop this behavior, nor did he try to find out which classmate stole my glasses. He had me change seats to sit in front of the room so that I can see the writing on the board. From this point on, I became enraged. I no longer smiled like I once did and I left no room or opportunity for a classmate to offend me in any way without it ending in me physically beating them. Sometimes I'd throw things at them for laughing too much because usually their bad behavior began after their laughs. I threw chairs in class, desks, hit children with rulers, start fights and beat them in class, I've done anything to get my peers to leave me alone. The teacher's way wasn't working, mine did! As a result of this, the gang of students became smaller in numbers because the message they received was that I did not care about the teacher, the class, or outcome and my intentions were to physically beat anyone who initiates. Hence, I, instilled fear.

I will end here because I can definitely go on and on about the different things that I had to deal with at school. At this time, I would like to explain how chronic torment has affected me and the development of my social emotional skills.

How I was effected:

1. Chronic Anger & Hostility
2. I developed anxiety because I was consistently under attack
3. I became Withdrawn, oftentimes shut down and wouldn't speak to anyone
4. I lost hope and respect for adults
5. Distrust people
6. Self-doubt and Self-Blame

7. I never expressed vulnerability or anything that troubled me

8. I wasn't fully expressive. There were two sides of me which I expressed most rage and my sense of humor. When I wasn't angry I was easy to laugh. Much of it is my personality and much of it was my way of escaping from the harshness of my reality.

Due to having these effects, here are a list of import social and personal skillsets which either receded or I did not have the opportunity to develop and why:

1. Healthy Self Esteem-> Confidence in one's own worth or abilities; self-respect:

The unloving and non-affirming environment I was in did not afford me the opportunity to learn what my worth and abilities were. I was confident and advocated for myself however, it came from a place of me knowing that I didn't do anything to cause such reactions and not standing for injustice against me. Not a place of knowing that I was worthy to be loved, respected and protected because I never was.

2. Social Skills-> Are the skills we use to communicate and interact with each other, both verbally and non-verbally, through gestures, body language

and our personal appearance. Human beings are sociable hence we have developed many ways to communicate our messages, thoughts and feelings with others. This includes:

Social Emotional Development which includes a child's experiences, expression, management of emotions and the ability to establish positive and rewarding relationships with others. Which also encompasses intra-personal process which deals with self-communication and the processes that involves perception of self and the inter-personal process which deals with one's ability to communicate with and relate to other people.

Listening Skills which is the ability to accurately receive and interpret messages in the communication process. This includes showing respect to the individual who is talking and the ability to identify and accurately perceive non-verbal communication.

3. How to Greet Others which includes making eye contact, how to introduce oneself, how to start a conversation, finding topics to discuss.

4. Following Instructions which is one's ability to act on requests by others, it requires a child to attend to details in speech, to sequence the information

in the appropriate steps and to seek clarification if they have trouble recalling information.

5. How to ask for Help which includes: Knowing there's a problem, knowing you need help, knowing who can help and getting help from them.

6. How to Disagree Respectfully which includes: Not taking things personal, avoid putting down other people's ideas and beliefs, Use I statements oppose to you statements, Listen to other point of views and staying calm.

7. How to Apologize, why and understand why apologizing is difficult for some children which includes being accountable, showing remorse for one's actions, acknowledge that one's actions have caused someone else harm.

8. How to accept rejection which includes teaching your child/children grit by comforting them and validating their experience, make failing safe, teaching them to try again if they don't succeed, tie your children's value to their character, not their achievements, leading and affirming them from the back.

But the hostile environment did not provide a safe and comfortable space for me to develop these Social Emotional skills which are like a team sport and require a team effort, respect and reciprocity from the people in the environment.

Some of these skills came natural to me hence, it was a matter of being around people who respected and liked me to actually see that I had a healthy outlook in those areas. However, i developed much of these skills when I became an adult and some of them are under developed still to this day.

Typically, many children who have had to cope with chronic and extreme bullying continue to struggle with building good relationships because it taught them to doubt themselves and when self-doubt sets in a child tend to lose confidence that they can achieve their goals. This also cause procrastination and indecisiveness. All do to the disadvantages of having healthy Social Emotional Skills. Some become adults who struggle to achieve goals that require working well with others because they are inadequate at identifying social ques.

Needless to say, I found the courage to fight in knowing that I am a human being and was entitled to the same education as my peers because I looked at everyone and asked myself, what made them more entitled than me to come to school and not be tormented and I couldn't find an answer. This was the foundation to my resilience, will to fight and confidence to stand up and speak out against what was happening to me!

I don't think teachers and school leadership understand the severe and complex role they play in how a child who is targeted perceive themselves, their peers, is perceived by their peers and the role they play in the confidence students develop to torment their peers without questioning themselves. How what they do or don't do, say or don't say and how they say it and do it determines the direction and energy of administration and pupils that attend the respective school. And these school years are a great part of the foundation of a child's life in which each child develop their ideology about themselves, people, life and leadership. An accountable, empathic, positive and optimistic spirit should be apart of any school's leadership and structure if you wish to see more children thrive with pure joy.

TABLE OF CONTENTS

First and foremost, I would like to thank my Ancestors and God for extending their grace, mercy and guidance upon me so that I was able to manifest this book with great purpose and my purest intentions for resolve.

I thank Nationwide Children's Hospital for allowing me to use them as a resource for this guide.

I thank my childhood friend for participating in the Q and A's and lending her perspective on this matter.

I thank Dawn Monique Edmond for her suggestions on some of the direction of this guide.

Author's photo credit Snapshots by TAI .

Below is an example of a child who was targeted. The purpose of tormenting Mallory was centered around assassinating her character and social status with the initial use of Cyber Bullying:

During Spring-Summer of 2016, Mallory Grossman of Rockaway Township, New Jersey was described as a vibrant 12-year-old who loved cheerleading and gymnastics. Mallory also made and sold jewelry to raise money for Camp Good Days, a summer camp for children with Cancer and children who have lost someone to cancer. By October of 2016 and the following nine months Mallory underwent Cyberbullying through Instagram posts, Snapchats and text messages. She was also tormented in her classrooms and the school hallways by a group of sixth grade girls. Mallory was told that she had no friends and that she was a loser. One of the girls asked Mallory "Why don't you kill yourself?" According to Mallory's parents, she complained of having headaches, her grades dropped and she begged to stay home from school. According to Mallory's parents, they spoke to teachers, counselors, school administrators and the students' parents however, the torment didn't cease. June 14, 2017, Mallory took her life. The type of death has not been revealed.

CHAPTER 1

Let's Talk Statistics, Facts & True Examples:

According to www.stopbullying.gov:

The two modes of bullying in\\+clude **direct** *(e.g.,* bullying that occurs in the presence of a targeted youth) and **indirect** *(e.g., bullying not directly communicated to a targeted youth such as spreading rumors). In addition to these two modes, the four types of bullying include broad categories of* **physical, verbal, relational** *(e.g.,* efforts to harm the reputation or relationships of the targeted youth), and **damage to property***.*

Electronic bullying or cyberbullying can also involve property damage resulting from electronic attacks that lead to the modification, dissemination, damage, or destruction of a youth's privately stored electronic information.

Some bullying can fall into criminal categories such as harassment, hazing, or assault.

December 2013, 19-year-old Chun Michael Deng, Pi Delta Psi of Baruch College in New York City died during a Pledge and hazing ritual. It is explained that Chun was blindfolded, wore a backpack loaded with 20 pounds of sand and was forced to run a gauntlet while fraternity brothers physically kept him from passing them by shoving him to the ground. During the ritual, Chun fell, hit his head and was immediately unconscious. According to the police report, fraternity members took Chun to the hospital 2 hours after the incident while others were told to protect the fraternity and hide all evidence. Forensic pathologist concluded that the 2-hour delay in bringing Chun to the hospital "significantly contributed to his death. The coroner's office determined that Chun died of closed head trauma, ruling Chun's death a homicide. January 2018 Pi Delta Psi Inc., a national fraternity was banned from operating in Pennsylvania for 10 years and have been charged with a fine of $112,500 for the hazing death of pledge Chun Michael Deng. On the same day, 4 ex Fraternity members have been sentenced to do time plus 7 years of probation.

According to American Society for the Care of Children:

About 28 percent of students ages 12–18 reported being bullied at school during the school year, according to the Indicators of School Crime and Safety: 2013 report, by the Bureau of Justice Statistics (BJS) and National Center for Education Statistics Institute of Education Sciences (IES). The majority of bullying still takes place at school; 1 in 3 U.S. students say they *have been bullied at school, according to the DHHS.*

It is reported in the CDC's Youth Risk Behavior Surveillance — 2013 report, that on average across 39 states survey, 7.2% (range: 3.6% – 13.1%) of students admit to not going to school due to personal safety concerns. Many dread the physical and verbal aggression of their peers, and many more attend school in a chronic state of anxiety and depression. *It's reported that 70.6% (footnote #12 or click "Show" under National Statistics)* of young people say they have seen bullying in their schools. While bullying can result in reluctance to go to school and truancy, headaches and stomach pains, reduced appetite, shame, anxiety, irritability, aggression and depression are also frequent effects.

"Children cannot get a quality education if they don't first feel safe at school."

-Arne Duncan, U.S. Secretary of Education

"160,000 kids per day do not attend school for fear of being bullied."

-U.S. Dept. of Justice

"The child who is overweight is the most likely to be bullied."

-Journal of Pediatrics

RISK FACTORS

No single factor puts a child at risk of being bullied or bullying others. Bullying can happen anywhere—cities, suburbs, or rural towns. Depending on the environment, some groups— such as <u>lesbian, gay, bisexual, or transgendered (LGBT) youth</u>, <u>youth with disabilities</u>, and socially isolated youth— may be at an increased risk of being bullied.

FEDERALLY COLLECTED DATA REPORTS

The 2011 Youth Risk Behavior Surveillance System (Centers for Disease Control and Prevention) indicates that 20% of students in grades 9–12 experienced bullying nationwide.

The 2008–2009 School Crime Supplement (National Center for Education Statistics and Bureau of Justice Statistics) indicates that 28% of students in grades 6–12 experienced bullying nationwide.

NATIONAL STATISTICS

- **BEEN BULLIED**

    28% of U.S. students in grades 6–12 experienced bullying.[9]

    20% of U.S. students in grades 9–12 experienced bullying.[10]

- **BULLIED OTHERS**

    Approximately 30% of young people admit to bullying others in surveys.[11]

- **SEEN BULLYING**

    70.6% of young people say they have seen bullying in their schools.[12]

    70.4% of school staff have seen bullying. 62% witnessed bullying two or more times in the last month and 41% witness bullying once a week or more.[13]

    When bystanders intervene, bullying stops within 10 seconds 57% of the time.[14]

- **BEEN CYBERBULLIED**

    6% of students in grades 6–12 experienced cyberbullying.[15]

    16% of high school students (grades 9–12) were electronically bullied in the past year.[16]

However, 55.2% of LGBT students experienced cyberbullying.[17]

According to National Voices for Equality, Education and Enlightenment:

1. *Every 7 MINUTES a child is bullied. Adult intervention – 4%. Peer intervention – 11%. No intervention – 85%.*
2. *Biracial and multiracial youth are more likely to be victimized than youth who identify with a single race.*
3. **Bullied students tend to grow up more socially anxious, with less self-esteem and require more mental health services throughout life.**
4. *Only 7% of U.S. parents are worried about cyberbullying; yet 33% of teenagers have been victims of cyberbullying*
5. *Kids who are obese, gay, or have disabilities are up to 63% more likely to be bullied than other children.*
6. ***1 MILLION** children were **harassed, threatened or subjected to other forms of cyberbullying on FACEBOOK** during the past year.*
7. *86% of students said, **"other kids picking on them, making fun of them or bullying them"** causes teenagers to turn to lethal violence in schools.*

8. *It is estimated that 160,000 children miss school every day due to fear of attack or intimidation by other students. Source: National Education Association.*

9. *American schools harbor approximately 2.1 million bullies and 2.7 million of their victims. Dan Olweus, National School Safety Center.*

Below is a Q&A that I've had with a childhood friend of Newark, NJ who experienced torment during the years we've attended elementary school:

Q. How old were you when you began to experience torment?

A. 5 Years old. I was in Kindergarten

Q. Did you tell anyone?

A. No because I thought everything would pass, but it didn't and I got tired of it after a while.

Q. Did any adult help?

A. No?

Q. Did anyone help you?

A. Yea, yourself helped me

Q. How did torment make you feel?

A. I was upset, frustrated, annoyed. It makes you feel bad.

Q. How did the torment start?

A. It starts with children making fun of you. They don't try to fight you in kindergarten. They made fun of my height.

Q. When did children start physical fights with you?

A. It started when I was in the 4th and 5th grades. When they wanted to fight me, it starts with pushing and shoving.

Q. How long have you been tormented?

A. I've been tormented for a long time. I would say 8 years.

Q. How did you feel about going to school?

A. It comes to a point where you don't wanna go to school to have to deal with kids throwing spit balls on you, etc...

More perspective from the interviewee:

"What's playing out today as far as the violence in school is how we were thinking back then! Something needs to be changed. They didn't see torment as a problem until somebody got hurt. They shouldn't wait until someone get hurt or killed before you see it as a problem. At a young age parents allow their kids to curse or laugh at someone. They don't see the problem that it can cause."

Q. Why did you continue to go to school?

A. I wanted my education and I knew there was a better life than what we were living.

Here is what the interviewee had to say in regards to President Trump's speech at the Conservative Political Action Conference back in February 2018, in which he was clear of his support of arming teachers with guns because he believe that schools will be safe. Per President Trump "when we declare our schools to be gun free zones, it just puts our students in far more danger."

Response from interviewee:

"What makes a child psycho? He may have been going through some things that they chose not to

handle. They chose to look the other way. It should never have to get to the point of where he think he has to kill somebody. Now they want to arm teachers with guns."

Quote from author:

"Arming teachers with guns creates another problem yet, they still haven't solved the initial problem."

Quote from interviewee:

"Parents need to be more involved with what their children are doing."

SUICIDE STATISTICS:

1. *Suicide remains among the leading causes of death of children under 14. In most cases, the young people die from hanging.*

2. *Suicide rates among 10 to 14-year-olds have grown more than 50 percent over the last three decades. (The American Association of Suicidology, AAS)*

3. *A new review of studies from 13 countries found signs of an apparent connection between bullying, being bullied, and suicide. (Yale School of Medicine)*

4. *Suicide rates among children between the ages of 10 & 14 are very low, but are "creeping up." (Ann Haas, Director of the Suicide Prevention Project at the American Foundation for Suicide Prevention)*

5. *The suicide rate among young male adults in Massachusetts rose 28 percent in 2007. However, that does not reflect deaths among teenagers and students Carl's age. (Massachusetts Dept. of Public Health, in a report released April 8, 2009)*

6. *Since 2002, at least 15 schoolchildren ages 11 to 14 have committed suicide in Massachusetts. Three of them were Carl's age. ("Constantly Bullied, He Ends His Life at Age 11," by Milton J. Valencia. The Boston Globe, April 20, 2009)*

7. *Suicide rates among 10 to 14-year-olds have grown more than 50 percent over the last three decades. (The American Association of Suicidology, AAS)*

8. *In 2005 (the last year nationwide stats were available), 270 children in the 10-14 age group killed themselves. (AAS)*

9. *1 in 7 Students in Grades K-12 is either a bully or a victim of bullying.*

10. *56% of students have personally witnessed some type of bullying at school.*

11. *15% of all school absenteeism is directly related to fears of being bullied at school.*

12. *71% of students report incidents of bullying as a problem at their school.*

13. *1 out of 20 students has seen a student with a gun at school.*

14. *282,000 students are physically attacked in secondary schools each month.*

15. *Those in the lower grades reported being in twice as many fights as those in the higher grades. However, there is a lower rate of serious violent crimes in the elementary level than in the middle or high schools.*

16. *90% of 4th through 8th graders report being victims of bullying.*

17. *Among students, homicide perpetrators were more than twice as likely as homicide victims to have been bullied by peers.*
18. *Bullying statistics say revenge is the strongest motivation for school shootings.*
19. *87% of students said shootings are motivated by a desire to "get back at those who have hurt them."*
20. *86% of students said, "other kids picking on them, making fun of them or bullying them" causes teenagers to turn to lethal violence in the schools.*
21. *61% of students said students shoot others because they have been victims of physical abuse at home.*
22. *54% of students said witnessing physical abuse at home can lead to violence in school.*
23. *According to bullying statistics, 1 out of every 10 students who drops out of school does so because of repeated bullying.*
24. *Harassment and bullying have been linked to 75% of school-shooting incidents.*

Read more about Carl Joseph Walker-Hoove here: http://www.masslive.com/news/index.ssf/2009/04/mom_says_springfield_boy_11_wh.html

In Aurora, Colorado 10 year-old Ashawnty Davis who was in the 5th grade have been tormented at school.

Ashawnty's parents describe her as being a happy girl until the end of October of 2017 which was when Ashawnty was involved in her first physical fight with the child who have been tormenting her. They learned that the fight was recorded by another student and posted on a social site which, according to her parents, caused Ashawnty much devastation. To the point that she took her own life two weeks afterwards. Ashawnty was found hanging in her closet. Her parents said that she was a victim of bullycide.

LGBT BULLYING STATISTICS

1. *In a 2007 study, 86% of LGBT students said that they had experienced harassment at school during the previous year. (Gay, Lesbian and Straight Education Network — GLSEN)*

2. *Research indicates that LGBT youth may be more likely to think about and attempt suicide than heterosexual teens. (GLSEN)*

3. *In a 2005 survey, students said their peers were most often bullied because of their appearance, but the next top reason was because of actual or perceived sexual orientation and gender expression. ("From Teasing to Torment: School Climate of America" — GLSEN and Harris Interactive)*

4. *According to the Gay, Lesbian and Straight Education Network 2007 National School Climate Survey of more than 6,000 students...*

5. *Nearly 9 out of 10 LGBT youth reported being verbally harassed at school in the past year because of their sexual orientation*

6. *Nearly half (44.1 percent) reported being physically harassed*

7. *About a quarter (22.1 percent) reported being physically assaulted.*

8. *Nearly two-thirds (60.8 percent) who experienced harassment or assault never reported the incident to the school*

9. *Of those who did report the incident, nearly one-third (31.1 percent) said the school staff did nothing in response*

10. *http://www.makebeatsnotbeatdowns.org/facts new.html*

Fallbrook, California, a 16-year-old transgender girl by the name of Taylor Alesana faced cyberbullying and torment at school. Though she faced torment, Alesana found a way to support and inspire other trans youth. In November of 2014, Alesana spoke at the Transgender Day of Remembrance regarding to the violence that trans people face and especially women of color. In which she stated "One in twelve transgender women are killed each year." Alesana then gave her own testament of what it is like to live as an out trans woman. She stated that she's usually alone and "being transgender, for me, means I've lost tons of friends...tons. It's been hell." According to the North County LGBTQ Resource Center executive, Alesana informed a school counselor of the torment she'd been facing but circumstances did not change. Alesana ended her life while on Spring break. Her family chose to keep the details about her death private.

CYBER BULLYING STATISTICS:

1. _32%_ of online teens say they have been **targets of a range of annoying or potentially menacing online activities**. _15% of teens overall say someone has forwarded or posted a private message they've written, 13% say someone has spread a rumor about them online, 13% say someone has sent them a threatening or aggressive message, and 6% say someone has posted embarrassing pictures of them online._

2. _38%_ of online **girls report being bullied**, _compared with 26% of online boys. In particular, 41% of older girls (15-17) report being bullied—more than any other age or gender group._

3. _39%_ of **social network users have been cyber bullied** in some way, compared with 22% of online teens who do not use social networks.

4. _20%_ of teens (12-17) say **"people are mostly unkind" on online social networks**. _Younger teenage girls (12-13) are considerably more likely to say this. One in three (33%) younger teen girls who use social media say that people their age are "mostly unkind" to one another on social network sites._

5. _15%_ of teens on social networks have experienced someone being **mean or cruel to them on a social network site**. *There are no statistically significant differences by age, gender, race, socioeconomic status, or any other demographic characteristic.*

6. _13%_ of teens who use social media (12-17) say they have had an experience on a social network that **made them feel nervous about going to school the next day**. *This is more common among younger teens (20%) than older teens (11%).*

7. _88%_ of social media-using teens say **they have seen someone be mean or cruel** to another person on a social network site. *12% of these say they witness this kind of behavior "frequently."*

8. When teens see others being mean or cruel on social networks, _frequently 55%_ see **other people just ignoring what is going on**, *27% see others defending the victim, 20% see others telling the offender to stop, and 19% see others join in on the harassment.*

9. _36%_ of teens who have witnessed others being cruel on social networks have **looked to someone for advice** about what to do.

10. _67%_ of all teens say bullying and harassment **happens more offline than online**.

11. _1 in 6 parents_ **know their child has been bullied over social media**. *In over half of these cases, their*

child was a repeat victim. Over half of parents whose children have social media accounts are concerned about cyberbullying and more than three-quarters of parents have discussed the issue of online bullying with their children.

12. _11%_ of middle school students were **victims of cyberbullying in the past two months**. *Girls are more likely than boys to be victims or bully/victims.*

13. **"Hyper-networking" teens** (those who spend more than three hours per school day on online social networks) are_110% morelikely_ to be a victim of cyberbullying, compared to those who *don't spend as much time on social networks.*

14. *95% of social media-using teens who have witnessed cruel behavior on social networking sites say they have seen others ignoring the mean behavior; 55% witness this frequently. (Pew Internet Research Center, FOSI, Cable in the Classroom, 2011):*

    1. *84% have seen the people defend the person being harassed; 27% report seeing this frequently.*

    2. *84% have seen the people tell cyberbullies to stop bullying; 20% report seeing this frequently.*

15. *66% of teens who have witnessed online cruelty have also witnessed others joining; 21% say they have also*

joined in the harassment. (Pew Internet Research Center, FOSI, Cable in the Classroom, 2011)

16. *Only 7% of U.S. parents are worried about cyberbullying, even though 33% of teenagers have been victims of cyberbullying (Pew Internet and American Life Survey, 2011)*

17. *85% of parent of youth ages 13-17 report their child has a social networking account. (American Osteopathic Association, 2011)*

18. *52% of parents are worried their child will be bullied via social networking sites. (American Osteopathic Association, 2011)*

19. *1 in 6 parents know their child has been bullied via a social networking site. (American Osteopathic Association, 2011)*

20. *One million children were harassed, threatend or subjected to other forms of cyberbullying on Facebook during the past year. (Consumer Reports, 2011)*

21. *43% of teens aged 13 to 17 report that they have experienced some sort of cyberbulying in the past year.*

22. *More girls are cyberbullys than boys (59% girls and 41% boys).*

23. *Cyberbullies spend more time online than other teens overall (38.4 hours compared to 26.8 hours).*

Tyler Clementi, former Rutgers University of Piscataway, NJ student recently came out to his parents that he was gay a couple of days prior to attending college. On September 19th, 2010 Tyler's roommate activated their computer web camera and recorded Tyler having a moment of intimacy with his male partner without Tyler's knowledge or consent, then posted about the recording on Twitter. Tyler's roommate encouraged friends and followers to view his webcam via Twitter thinking that he would record another act of intimacy between Tyler and his male partner but it didn't happen at that time. Tyler later found out about the recording and tweets and on September 22, 2010 Tyler Clementi jumped from the George Washington Bridge to his death.

School Violence STATISTICS:

- *100,000 students carry a gun to school each day*
- *28% of youths who carry weapons have witnessed violence at home*
- *Among students, homicide perpetrators were more than twice as likely as homicide victims to have been bullies by peers.*
- *More youth violence occurs on school grounds as opposed to on the way to school.*
- *1/3 of students surveyed said they heard another student threaten to kill someone.*

Teachers & Bullying:

- *Teachers are also assaulted, robbed & bullied. 84 crimes per 1,000 teachers per year.*

References:

- **Bureau of Justice Statistics – School Crime & Safety**

Fast Facts Chart According to National Center for Education Statistics:

Percentage of students ages 12–18 who reported being bullied at school during the school year, by type of bullying and ex: 2015

NOTE: «At school» includes in the school building, on school property, on a school bus, and going to and from school. Students who reported experiencing more than one type of bullying at school were counted only once in the total for students bullied at school.

May 7th, 2013 Dr. Louise Ingram Royal, teacher at Seminole County Elementary School in Donalsonville, GA was assaulted by a parent which was caught on the school surveillance. The parent was seen on camera repeatedly kicking, beating and hitting Dr. Royal with a custodial broom. Dr. Royal suffered irreversible brain damage, injuries to her jaw and arm and she lost sight in her right eye. December, 2013 a jury found the parent guilty of the following charges: Aggravated Assault, aggravated battery, terrorist threats and disturbing a school. The sentenced the parent to 35 years in jail and she must serve at least 20 years.

March of 2011 in Irvington, NJ, Muideen Oladoja, an Algebra teacher at Irvington High School had been punched in the face by a 15-year old student, then dragged out of his classroom into the hallway where he was attacked and beaten by a total of 5 high school students which was caught on school surveillance cameras. Muideen Oladoja was taken to a local hospital where he was treated for unspecified injuries.

Per Ethel J. Hasty, Irvington High School's Superintendent those 5 students have been expelled from Irvington High School. She also advised that there were other options so that those students can continue their education within the district, with classes taught in the evening, etc...

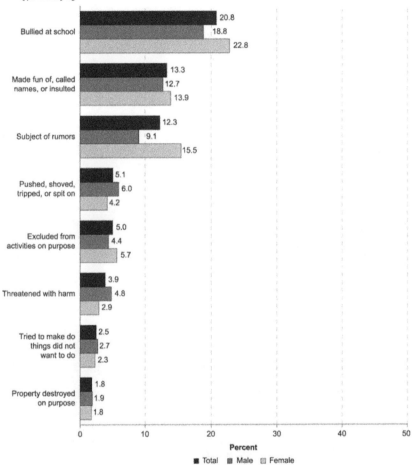

Type of bullying

Type of bullying	Total	Male	Female
Bullied at school	20.8	18.8	22.8
Made fun of, called names, or insulted	13.3	12.7	13.9
Subject of rumors	12.3	9.1	15.5
Pushed, shoved, tripped, or spit on	5.1	6.0	4.2
Excluded from activities on purpose	5.0	4.4	5.7
Threatened with harm	3.9	4.8	2.9
Tried to make do things did not want to do	2.5	2.7	2.3
Property destroyed on purpose	1.8	1.9	1.8

Percent

■ Total　▩ Male　▨ Female

CHAPTER 2

Let's Talk Effects of Torment aka Bullying

According to www.Pacer.org:
Effects of Bullying

- Students who experience bullying are at increased risk for poor school adjustment, sleep difficulties, anxiety, and depression (**Center for Disease Control, 2015**).
- Students who are both targets of bullying and engage in bullying behavior are at greater risk for both mental health and behavior problems than students who only bully or are only bullied (**Center for Disease Control, 2015**).
- Bullied students indicate that bullying has a negative effect on how they feel about themselves (19%), their relationships with friends and family and on their school work (14%), and physical health

(9%) (**National Center for Educational Statistics, 2016).**

- Students who experience bullying are twice as likely as non-bullied peers to experience negative health effects such as headaches and stomachaches (**Gini & Pozzoli, 2013**).
- Youth who self-blame and conclude they deserved to be bullied are more likely to face negative outcomes, such as depression, prolonged victimization, and maladjustment **(Perren, Ettakal, & Ladd, 2013;)**.

Other effects of Torment for the tormented

- The tormented can develop extreme Sadness
- The tormented can develop mood Swings – an abrupt and apparent unaccountable change of mood.
- The tormented can develop a lack of confidence
- The tormented may lose their appetite
- The tormented may develop an Influx of appetite
- The tormented can become a heavy sleeper (difficulty waking up from sleep)
- The tormented may develop a lack of personal hygiene and self-care
- The tormented can develop forgetfulness
- The tormented can become withdrawn

- The tormented may develop helplessness-> They believe that they cannot do anything to help themselves
- The tormented can develop hopelessness-> They believe that results will not be in their best interest
- The tormented may develop anxiety-> They're afraid and worry about what can/will happen
- The tormented cease to build bonds and friendships
- The tormented lose friends
- The tormented may wet the bed (depends on their age)
- The tormented may become a bully
- The tormented may have poor school grades
- The tormented can develop extreme silliness, everything becomes a joke as a way to escape their reality
- The tormented can develop an anti-social personality disorder
- The tormented can become a narcissist
- The tormented may develop paranoia
- The tormented can become indecisive
- The tormented may cease to have courage
- The tormented may experience headaches or migraines

- The tormented may experience muscle pain
- The tormented may experience a change in the function of their immune system

Effects of Torment for the Tormentor:

- The tormentor becomes domineering
- The tormentor develops a deliberate lack of patience
- The tormentor develops a deliberate lack of understanding
- The tormentor becomes Self-Opinionated
- The tormentor develops a curt persona even if that's not who they truly are because they are allowed to be who they are without a challenge
- The tormentor think that they are always right because they defy logic which differs from their own
- The tormentor becomes irrational
- The tormentor becomes narcissistic
- The tormentor can later become a psychopath (a type of antisocial personality disorder diagnosed for adults)
- The tormentor becomes self-entitled
- The tormentor lack accountability
- The tormentor develops a lack of empathy

Looking at the effects of the tormented, we will also find that the tormented child's mental state is in a consistent state of emergency, panic, and fear because they are constantly under attack, do not feel safe, or peace. This environment and state of being also contribute to excessive thinking, worrying and excessive breathing which in turn creates an over worked heart, brain and nervous system. This level of stress is unhealthy for a child or any human being to endure on a consistent basis, it aides in the deterioration of the body and immune system depending on the intensity, length of events and the child's perspective of themselves and their environment. Also, such merciless environment does not allot for most growing children to develop into the truest, most confident expression of themselves. Having lasting effects into adulthood which aid in shaping the kind of adult they become. It is understood that many adults, including myself have had some unpleasant experiences during our childhood and adolescent years that we have had no control over which along with our personal beliefs and principles has shaped us and is apart of who we are however, School Torment can and should be avoided.

Think about this the next time someone repeat: "They are just being kids."

Let's continue. Looking at the effects of the tormentor, we will also learn that the tormentor oftentimes, blow things out of proportion. If they think or feel that they have been wronged, their retaliation oftentimes is disproportionate to what was done that made them feel hurt. They also believe that they have the right to retaliate every time they think that they've been wronged. A challenge here is that they think everything that they do is right because it is right in their favor. The other challenge is that they do not see or understand that their initial actions hurt others or have a negative impact on their family members and living circumstance. Meanwhile, they know that their retaliation hurt others because it is their intent. Hence, they do not think that they should be challenged or not allowed to have their way. Also, they do not develop a sense of remorse for their wrong actions because in their mind, it is someone else fault. Someone else is the reason why they retaliate in the way that they do.

Children who behave this way also fall within the Conduct Disorder sector and they develop a false sense of confidence and what is wrong and right because they have not been strategically challenged in a way which provokes them to think about why they behave in the way that they do, should they behave in such way and to what degree. They must also be challenged to think about how others are affected in ways that they don't quite see or understand so that they can understand that their actions affect more than what they know and understand. When conventional methods do not work, it is time to learn and apply new methods. If not, parents, teachers and guardians will experience frustration and at times feel like giving up. Then, the subliminal message here is that your child can do what they want, even if it hurt others and get away with it and that there is nothing anyone can do to encourage them to consider doing things a different way. In turn, this encourages a child who torment others to look for or create similar circumstances because they feel powerful, get attention and get their way within circumstances that are disadvantages for their peers. Also, this aids in the tormentor's inability to be remorseful for results which are unhealthy for others that is caused by their plot and implementation. Enabling them to develop a character of moral corruptness and lack of empathy because their intentions are to perform acts for personal gain even if it is at the expense of other people. The question here is, what kind of adult will they become?

Consider this the next time someone repeat: "kids will be kids."

A great book to read that can help in this aspect was written by Dr. Shefali Tsabary called: The Conscious Parent transforming ourselves empowering our children. Dr. Shefali was invited on Oprah's Life Class in May 2014 where it was the first time that I have heard of her and her perspective. Dr. Shefali's beliefs on parenting skills and the basis for writing this book are as follows:

"Instead of merely being the receiver of the parents' psychological and physical legacy, children function as ushers of the parents' development. Parents unwittingly pass on an inheritance of psychological pain and emotional shallowness. To handle the behavior that results, the traditional books on parenting abound with clever techniques for control and quick fixes for dysfunction. In Dr. Shefali Tsabary's conscious approach to parenting, however, children serve as mirrors of their parents' forgotten self. Those willing to look in the mirror have an opportunity to establish a relationship with their own inner state of wholeness. Once they find their way back to their essence, parents enter into communion with their children, shifting away from the traditional parent-to-child "know it all" approach and more towards a mutual parent-with-children relationship. The pillars of the parental ego crumble as the parents awaken the ability of their children to transport them into a state of presence."

The "ah hah" moment!

Other great books to read that were written by Dr. Shefali Tsabary are: The Awakened Family How to Raise Empowered, Resilient and Conscious Children and Out of Control Why disciplining your child doesn't work... and what will.

CHAPTER 3

Let's Talk Character and Personality Disorders

Let's dig a little deep. During my research I've learned that there is a condition called **_Alexithymia_** which is a personality construct characterized by the subclinical inability to identify and describe emotions in the self. The core characteristics of **_Alexithymia_** are marked dysfunction in emotional awareness, social attachment and interpersonal relating. **_Subclinical_** meaning relating to or denoting a disease that is not severe enough to present definite or readily observable symptoms. *"It's important to recognize that alexithymia isn't a diagnosis, but rather a construct used to describe someone that demonstrates the inability to understand or articulate his or her feelings. Someone affected by alexithymia literally cannot put words to their feelings, despite the desire to do so. It's difficult for someone with alexithymia to relate to his or her own experiences or even grasp the experiences of others. This* *can be frustrating for everyone – for those lacking in their emotional response and for those expecting an emotional response."*

Alexithymia can and may play a role in all three categories: The tormented, the tormentor and the bystander. If they are unable to understand and articulate their pain and discomfort, how will they know if they are tormenting someone? Are they able to identify torment? Can they help resolve?

The brain's **_Amygdala_**. According to the National Institute of Mental Health aka NIH the callous, unemotional characteristics of some children and adolescents who bully or steal or have severely disruptive behavior problems may have partial roots in a brain area called the **_Amygdala_**. The **_Amygdala_** responds to distress cues from other people; cues that normally would elicit empathy from observers. But it is less responsive to such cues in youth who have both callous, unemotional characteristics and disruptive behavior problems, report NIMH investigator Abigail Marsh, Ph. D., and colleagues. Results of this research appeared online in the American Journal of Psychiatry. It is important that you understand not all youth who have disruptive behavior problems have callous, unemotional characteristics. But in those who do, behavior problems tend to be more severe and persistent, per previous studies.

Digging deeper. Research also shows that there is a condition called **_Conduct Disorder_** _"which is a serious behavioral and emotional disorder that can occur in children and teens. A child with this disorder may display a pattern of disruptive and violent behavior and have problems following rules. It is not uncommon for children and teens to have behavior-related problems at some time during their development. However, the behavior is considered to be a_ **_Conduct Disorder_** _when it is long-lasting and when it violates the rights of others, goes against accepted norms of behavior and disrupts the child's or family's everyday life."_ If there are no intervention and or preventive action taken, what we witness as **_Conduct Disorder_** in children and teens can and will escalate to the personality traits/ mental conditions in adults known as: **_Antisocial Personality Disorder_** which include: **_Sociopathy_** & **_Psychopathy_** which are associated with the following personality traits respectively: **_Interpersonal Traits_**, **_Affective Traits_** and **_Lifestyle Traits_**. All of which you can learn more of in my upcoming book: **_Workplace Torment the Fade to Black Guide_** as these traits specifically pertain to adults. However, when examining characteristics and finding reasons why some children lack **_Empathy_** and **_Remorse_**, it is important that we look into

Conduct Disorder. According to WebMD Symptoms of Conduct Disorder vary depending on the age of the child and whether the disorder is mild, moderate, or severe. In general, symptoms of Conduct Disorder fall into four general categories:

- **Aggressive Behavior:** These are behaviors that threaten or cause physical harm and may include fighting, bullying, being cruel to others or animals, using weapons, and forcing another into sexual activity.
- **Destructive Behavior:** This involves intentional destruction of property such as arson (deliberate fire-setting) and vandalism (harming another person's property).
- **Deceitful Behavior:** This may include repeated lying, shoplifting, or breaking into homes or cars in order to steal.
- **Violation of Rules:** This involves going against accepted rules of society or engaging in behavior that is not appropriate for the person's age. These behaviors may include running away, skipping school, playing pranks, or being sexually active at a very young age.

In addition, many children with ***Conduct Disorder*** are irritable, have low self-esteem, and tend to throw frequent temper tantrums. Some may abuse drugs and alcohol. Children with Conduct Disorder often are unable to appreciate how their behavior can hurt others and generally have little guilt or remorse about hurting others.

For more on causes of Conduct Disorder and other Behavioral Health information, services, preventive methods and referrals, contact *Nationwide Children's at 614-722-2000*. This hospital has a record of parents who report to this location with their children for behavioral health and other services nationwide.

CHAPTER 4

Let's Talk Cause of Torment

The Tormented

Although there is absolutely no reason which makes it okay for some children to target and torment others, it is imperative that we take a look at some reasons why some children are targeted.

- The tormented may be extremely tall for their age group or small for their age group
- The tormented may be overweight or underweight
- The tormented may be from a different culture
- The tormented may be bi-cultural or bi-racial
- The tormented may wear glasses
- The tormented may have views that are uniquely different to their peers
- The tormented may have a different religion from their peer group

- The tormented may have a disability
- The tormented may be gay or lesbian
- The tormented may be popular
- The tormented may have a high IQ for their age
- The tormented may be perceived to be very attractive
- The tormented may have mood swings
- The tormented may be easily angered
- The tormented may be a victim of neglect, sexual molestation or other forms of child abuse and trauma in which the child's disposition most likely is a reflection of their state of mind which is crisis and self-preservation.
- The tormented may live in a domestic violence circumstance in which the child's disposition most likely is a reflection of their state of mind which is and self-preservation
- The tormented may live in a violent community where people that they know or are connected to in some way may have been badly hurt or lost their lives to violence. The child's disposition most likely is a reflection of their state of mind of grief, fear, anger and or bewilderment
- The tormented may be growing up impoverished and or neglected where they see themselves at a disadvantage to their peers, this may cause the child

to withdraw or act arrogant and over confident to compensate for their disadvantages

A child who is in any of these categories will become an easy target and may be tormented because they are either misunderstood or not respected yet vastly noticed. Already coping with a great deal of pressure due to their environment or differences, add torment, what do you think happens to that child's mental health, physical health and nervous system? Research explains that when we are exposed to stress such as torment, a chain of physical changes known as the fight or flight response are triggered within our bodies. This response is designed to enable us to protect ourselves from danger. When our brains determine a stressful situation, it stimulates the release of a hormone that encourages your kidneys to release adrenaline. Which triggers the release of the stress hormone called cortisol *(a steroid hormone that regulates a wide range of processes throughout the body, including metabolism and the immune response. It also has a very important role in helping the body respond to stress)*, the body's natural alert system which in turn, raises the body's blood pressure and pulse, increases the body's blood sugar levels and prepares the body's muscles for action while suppressing the immune and digestive functions. Although these natural functions aid to our ability to protect ourselves, when triggered on a consistent basis due to torment and trauma it creates physical and mental effects such as:

- Headaches or migraines
- Depression
- Muscle pain

Revert to page 10 for effects of the tormented.

It is understood that most parents want to see their children as good beings and being their best however, that is not realistic if parents are not preparing and teaching their children how to confidently advocate for themselves and have healthy self-esteem especially if they have physical or character differences. Also, it is imperative that parents understand that your children are effected by their environment and that environment, if not a safe haven has a negative mental, emotional and physical impact on your child or children. This also effects your child's ability to focus on their education in which poor grades will be the result. Also, what may make your child or children different is what other children may perceive to be a disadvantage or an advantage. Any child that is perceived at a disadvantage or an advantage is liable to be a target by children who choose to target them. You cannot control how your child is perceived by others however, you can help your child build a well-rounded, balanced and confident character. Here are some helpful suggestions:

- ❖ Register your child or children in a Self Defense program-> Besides learning physical defense, here is where their motor skills will improve which will increase their confidence. They will develop better communication, listening and social skills. They learn non-violent conflict resolution skills and much more.

- ❖ Sign them up to volunteer in their community-> They will develop a sense of accountability, they will develop good decision making skills, sense of service to help others and purpose. This experience or similar experiences allows children to connect with people with a sense of self-authority

- ❖ Appreciate the process and be supportive-> regardless of the outcome of any task, acknowledge their effort, take time to analyze and discuss their efforts, their strategy and what they can do to have a better outcome provided that a better outcome is needed. This process allows children to learn who they are intimately and learn the value of their input. This process will also develop and strengthen their self-worth.

❖ Should your attempts to resolve do not work or if you should feel that you are not taken serious concerning your child/children safety and education, you should consider transferring your child/children out of their current school and have them placed at a school that practice better proactive, preventive and intervention methods.

❖ Should all methods above not work, I strongly recommend that you consider home schooling your child/children.

Parents, it is important to remember that everything that happens in a child's life has lasting effects, well into their adult years. The types of effects and the type of adult your child becomes has a lot to do with their personal beliefs compiled with childhood trauma and other experiences. Hence, it is imperative that you provide your children with the best information and education. Help them develop their best problem solving skills, communication skills, their best negotiation skills, their best strategies, their best interpersonal skills, their best intrapersonal skills, their best self-advocacy skills and more. When your child/children have a positive wealth of information of self, there is no challenge they cannot overcome. #SelfWealth. The great news about this paradigm shift is that it's a win-win because parents, you'll find that you learn more about yourself during this process as well.

I wish you the best during this journey!

The Tormentor

Although there is no reason which makes it ok for a child to torment others, it is imperative that we look into some reason why this behavior takes place in our schools and communities.

- The tormentor may be a victim of neglect, sexual molestation or other forms of child abuse and trauma in which the child's disposition most likely is a reflection of their state of mind which is crisis, self-preservation, cynicism, rage and or anger.
- The tormentor may live in a domestic violence circumstance in which the child's disposition most likely is a reflection of their state of mind
- The tormentor may live in a violent community where people that they know or are connected to in some way may have been badly hurt or lost their lives to violence. The child's disposition most likely is a reflection of their state of mind of grief, fear, anger and or rage
- The tormentor may have been a victim of torment at school
- The tormentor may have views or characteristics that are uniquely different to their peers

- The tormentor may not like the target, a case of Personality Conflict-> When two or more people find themselves in conflict not over a particular issue or incident, but due to a fundamental incompatibility in their personalities, their approaches to things, or their style of life.
- The tormentor may be envious or jealous of the target where torment is the result
- The tormentor may not know how to express themselves or disagree with peers without resulting to violence
- The tormentor may use torment as a strategy to gain power or popularity
- The tormentor may be a child who falls within the Conduct Disorder or other Personality Disorder revert to pages 14 and 15
- The tormentor may be growing up impoverished and or neglected where they see themselves at a disadvantage to their peers. This may cause the child to become abusive or act arrogant and over confident to compensate for their disadvantages

The type of advice I have read on how to deal with torment/bullying fail to teach the tormented child true self development and fail to address the tormentor's true intentions and actions. E.g.:

- Ignore the tormentor/bully, walk away. This is a positive step however, this advice fail to acknowledge that plenty of tormented children ignore and walk away from tormentors only to have the tormentor consistently torment them for long periods of time like weeks, months, or the entire school year even. How does this advice stop the action of torment?

- Control your temper, walk away from the bully or use humor which is said to throw a bully off guard. It seems more like this method is teaching a tormented child how to walk away from issues that approach them that they must learn how to solve and how to make light of serious issues and people who pose a threat to their existence without the understanding that if said issue is not resolved, it will continue to be an issue in their lives. Although one must control their temper, how does this method help a child understand and deal with their emotions, the frustrations, anger and uncertainty that comes with being tormented?

- Do not fight back. It is said that the child that fights back reveals their anger, that they are liable to get hurt by responding physically because aggressive responses can lead to more violence and more torment for the victims. It is also said that friends of the tormented tend to stop associating with the victim when they retaliate with violence. The challenge I see with this method is that it teaches the tormented child that showing anger is showing weakness and that they can be manipulated by their anger. It teaches a child how to be afraid of the bully's response to their response for self-justice. Teaches the tormented child that if they want to keep their friends and associates, they should not respond to a tormentor with violence. Ultimately, this method teaches a tormented child that everyone who surrounds their situation is more important than them even though they are not directly affected by the treachery that comes with being tormented.

- Notify a teacher or other adult at school, that adult will find ways to help resolve the bullying. Only for a child to learn that solutions are not effective or to no avail. Simply because many adults believe that torment is apart of growing up, that kids will be kids, that kids don't have real problems and that they don't know anything about having problems and that getting tormented builds character. The challenge I see here is that adults compare their problems to those of children and say those are minor issues. Failing to realize that the problems children face at their age is equivalent to the problems adults face at their age. If we allow ourselves the gift of unbiased understanding, we will find that our problems coincide with our age and circumstances. Hence, a child who deals with torment goes through the same emotions and worry as an adult who struggles to make ends meet, or the adult who strategizes to be their best on their jobs so that they don't get fired or demoted. We must also question what do people mean when they say torment builds character. What type of character does torment build for the tormented and for the tormentor? What do we hope that the tormented child learn from this experience? Also, what do we hope that the tormentor learn from this experience?

It is imperative that adults understand that these messages actually teach children to accept imbalance, injustice and mistreatment rather than teach them how to thrive should the same cross their paths in life. In this case, it is important that we remember a golden rule which states "There is more than one way to skin a cat" and that we have the power to choose the way which best benefit all that is involved. If not, we will aid in the development of children who may have defeatist personalities, some suicidal, some un-empathetic, some indifferent, some vengeful, some narcissistic, etc...

who will go as far as to commit murder/homicide if effective preventive actions aren't implemented. Very few having developed social intelligence which determines their success with getting along with their peers, including tormentors. Or balance and empathy. Beg to differ? Well let's look at some examples of violence, bullycide and tragedies which either involves a torment situation or children/teens with Conduct Disorder, Anti-Social Personality Disorder, or other types of Physical or Mental Disorders:

CHAPTER 5

School Shootings Bullycide and Tragedies

In the United States

- Columbine High School Massacre-date occurred 4-20-1999, State Occurred CO-> 15 students killed 21 were injured
- Heritage High School Shooting-date occurred 5-20-1999, State occurred GA-> 6 students were injured
- Santana High School Shooting-date occurred 3-5-2001, State Occurred CA-> 2 students were killed 13 were injured
- Red Lake Indian Reservation/Red Lake Senior High Shootings-date occurred 3-21-2005, State occurred MN-> 10 people were killed 7 were injured
- Virginia Tech Massacre-date occurred 4-16-2007, State occurred VA-> 33 people were killed 23 were injured

- Sandy Hook Elementary School Shooting-date occurred 12-14-2012, State occurred CT-> 28 people students were killed 2 were injured
- Umpqua Community College Shooting-date occurred 10-1-2015, State occurred OR-> 10 people were killed 9 were injured
- Marshall County High School Shooting-date occurred 1-23-2018, state occurred KY-> 2 people were killed 18 were injured
- Marjory Stoneman Douglas High School Shooting-date occurred 2-14-2018, State occurred FL-> 17 people were killed 17 people were injured

Do note that there is a more extensive list of school shootings in various states on Wikipedia

Now, let us look at a list of Bullycide-> Suicide as a result of school torment

- 10/2011, Chilton, AL-> 12-year-old Dajia Lee committed bullycide by hanging herself.
- 7/13/2013, Arizona-> 17-year-old Carlos Vigil took his life as a result of dealing with torment since the 3rd grade
- 12/7/2010, Little Rock, AR-> 16-year-old Chandler Barnwell committed bullycide by shooting himself

- 11-28-2017, Yucaipa, CA-> Rosalie Avila, who was 13 years old, hung herself after years of torment. After Rosalie's death, her parents became victims of cyber bullying by those that tormented Rosalie and their family members
- 12/4/2017-> Thompson, CT-> 15-year-old Connor Francis Tronerud committed bullycide because of cyber torment
- 2/22/2016-> Dayton, ID-> 17-year-old Cassandra Porter committed bullycide
- 2/3/2018-> Hanover, PA-> 14 –year-old Bryan Doll hung himself as a result of cyber torment
- 3/2012-> Morristown, NJ-> 15-year-old Lennon Baldwin hung himself as a result of school torment. His parents sued. In 2018 New Jersey District will pay $625,000 to the parents of Lennon Baldwin

CHAPTER 6

Let's Talk Cultural Humility

Which is the ability to maintain an interpersonal stance that is open to the other in relation to aspects of cultural identity that are most important to the person. Cultural Humility focuses on self-humility rather than achieving a state of knowledge or awareness. Cultural Humility also encourages reflection and growth around culture in order to increase understanding and respect for cultural differences.

This is a very important factor. For me, being bi-cultural was a huge part of why I was targeted and tormented as a child and in my adolescent years, i found that it was very difficult to build comradery and friendships. My peers were more concerned with rejecting and condemning me because of my differences rather than notice that I am human, wanted to be loved and belonged as they wanted. Well I grew up in the 80's which were different times.

I mention that to inform you all that I fought and was hard to beat, for my spirit would not have allowed me to be pummeled by my peers. I understand that these are different times but in my day the only way to beat extreme torment was to beat the tormentors! I was labeled a trouble maker and a bad apple however, I built my mental resilience to the point where I couldn't care less of what my peers and school staff thought of me. I tried to talk things out however, that did not work because I was not respected as a peer. I also remember is that there wasn't a school staff or school guard who defended me, not one. I also had to make sure that my younger sister was safe at school as well. I knew in my little mind at that time, that if I didn't win those battles, my sister and I would have never been safe to continue going to school because we would get pummeled every day by groups of children. Again, my spirit would not have allowed me to not fight for my God given right to an education that my peers comfortably attended school to achieve.

I suggest researching games and books that teach Cultural Humility and select what best resonates with your family.

CHAPTER 7

Let's Try Empathy

Empathy is the ability to understand and share the feelings of another.

I have learned that in order to put myself in someone else's shoes, I must know what it feels like to walk in my own shoes. This means that I must understand my emotions and thoughts and understand why I feel and think the way I do. What I need to do in order to prevent a similar situation from happening and what I need to do to balance my emotions and thoughts. The foundation to doing this all begins with recognizing when I feel emotions and when thoughts arise that may encourage me to react in unpleasant ways towards others.

I suggest researching games and books that enlighten on empathy and select what best resonates with your family.

In closing I encourage us all to remember that the core spirit of our children today is what our future will reflect which also will determine how the future will treat us. They will be our future decision makers, policy makers, disciplinary, community activists, parents, teachers, retailers, law enforcement agents, you name it. What type of energy would you want the world to have in the future in which you believe you can feel comfortable growing old in?

CPSIA information can be obtained
at www.ICGtesting.com
Printed in the USA
BVHW032257120219
540122BV00001B/15/P